UNSHACKLED

WRITTEN BY: SANA MALIM
DESIGN & CONCEPT BY: OMER MALIM

To all our heroes and all our martyrs,
may peace and blessings be upon you,
wherever you go.

Special Thanks,
Nabeel Ahmad

A Note From The Author

Many of us believed that we would never be the same after seeing in real-time, a genocide take place on our screens. We all processed the shock, the distress, and the pain in different ways.

I wrote in my journal. I wrote what I thought, what I felt, what I was learning, and what I wanted to say to the monsters inflicting such evil. Still, a void filled my heart, and I asked myself, what more can I do for the people of Palestine?

This book is the answer to that question. I've written these reflections to relieve myself of the burdensome guilt that has been plaguing my mind, reminding me, that more should have been done to stop this madness. I've written these reflections to keep the lessons we've all learned alive, and to continue fighting for the truth. Most importantly, I've written these reflections as a means to raise funds for those who have lost everything in this senseless war on humanity.

I am forever grateful for your support.
Thank you, from the depths of my heart.

With Love,

Sana Malim

U N S H A C K L E D

The light cannot be shackled
no matter how hard you try
it will creek through the walls of every home you steal
the bark of every olive tree you burn
it will seep through the grains of soil
upon which martyrs lay
it will fill the views of all your sights
reminding you
the light cannot be shackled
no matter how hard you try.

UNSHACKLED

When hell devours the earth
and heaven begins to call for its people
read the verses aloud and say
this is the story of
resistance from occupation.

UNSHACKLED

When the truth is silenced
it becomes louder
untameable
spreading like wildfire
leaving the essence of every being in its path
exposed
until
one either burns with the flames
or extinguishes it
and then there remains
only the raging truth.

UNSHACKLED

Do they see
that the soil of their claimed holy land
has become barren?
drenched with the blood of
God's most sacred -
the blood of infants?
that the air echoes the agonizing cries of
burning children?

U N S H A C K L E D

When justice can no longer
be fulfilled on earth
know that you have surpassed
the height of evil.

UNSHACKLED

One day
they will come to realize
that every drop of blood
shed from a martyr's blessed body
was a curse on their life
and a testament of their evil
when all stand
before the Almighty.

UNSHACKLED

For a life of sixty
seventy
maybe eighty years
they sell their souls
reigning hell on earth
without a second thought
that the same demons
they unleash on the world
will one day come for them too.
.

You can't escape
their resistance
if they can't escape
your oppression.

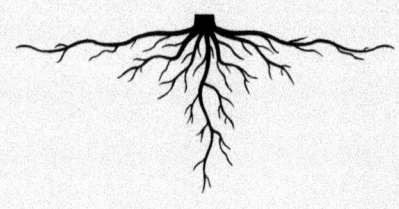

UNSHACKLED

God's chosen people
you were supposed to be the best of us
the epitomes of
mercy
humility
and justice
spreading peace and love throughout the earth
but here you are
dropping bombs from the sky
spilling blood like water
sentencing entire childhoods to die.

UNSHACKLED

When you mercilessly kill children
in the tens of thousands
when you starve them on the streets
when you deprive them of a future
and you do that for almost
eighty years
you prove to the world
why resistance was born
why resistance was necessary
and why resistance will prevail.

SANA MALIM
| 16 |

UNSHACKLED

You thought you were taking everything from them
freedom, dignity, hopes, dreams, family
even sustenance
but with nothing more left to lose
you made them a people
of courage
of faith
of power
of strength
who are
undefeatable
invincible
unconquerable
and that is why
you will always lose
in every version of this story.

The state of a believer is
always grateful
always hopeful
no matter what the eyes see
no matter what the heart feels.

It took a genocide to teach us that.

.

UNSHACKLED

People say religion is the cause of bloodshed
that religion is the root of all evil
but do you think Netanyahu has a god?
do you think Biden has a god?
I'd say no
but then
I'd say yes
because
power
money
and greed
are their gods
nothing holy would ever accept them
and that hunger
that thirst
has always been the root of all evil.

UNSHACKLED

And lately
I've been thinking
if these
are the people of jannah
if this
is the cost of jannah
what hope do I have
with my weak imaan and my weak tawakkul?

But then
I look at the leaders of this world
and I think
if these are the people of jahannum
with all of their wickedness
their brutality
their hypocrisy
then surely
my Lord will have mercy on me.

UNSHACKLED

I will never forget the man
who held his dead child in his arms
and cried out to the world

"I will be your opposition on the Day of Judgement."

.

UNSHACKLED

I keep asking myself
if a calamity were to befall me
would I be like the people of Falasteen?
would I be as resilient as them?
as courageous as them?
as confident in my victory, my success, as them?
would I be as satisfied with the qadr of Allah, as them?
with Alhumdulilah on my lips?
Hasbunallah Wa Ni'mal Wakeel, my first words?
would I remember Innallaaha Ma'As Sabireen?
or would I lose
my sense of self, my will to live, to survive, to thrive?
would I wait to die?
would I complain and question Allah's decree?
would I lose my imaan, my everything in the process?

I have never been so terrified to think
what if
                    what if
                                    what if
amidst the temporary suffering of this world
I would not be
like the people of Falasteen?

.

UNSHACKLED

Some nights
I imagine I'm a mother
living, breathing, surviving in Gaza
trying to come up with the words I would use
to explain to my child
why suddenly our homes, clothes, things are gone
why death lurks in every second of every day
why all our time is spent
moving from place to place
for food, for water, for shelter from the cold.

I've come up with a story
that I try to read aloud:

There are beasts that fly in the sky
and roam the streets at night
beasts that live over the wall
and become fiercer in the dark
every so often
they come out hungrier and thirstier
than the years that came before
but they are not to be feared
because fear is reserved only for Allah
and though they appear very big
they crumble with each passing day
falling lower and lower
into incessant pits below the earth
until even their limbs confess
they deserve every second of Allah's eternal wrath
when it finally manifests.

Some nights
I imagine I'm a mother
breathing, living, surviving in Gaza.

SANA MALIM

UNSHACKLED

In the midst of destruction
you lay down your prayer mat
fully aware
of bombs dropping
the bleeding bodies around you
you see
hear
feel
death everywhere
and yet you stand
raising your hands
to say Allah Hu Akbar
while I wither away
then break apart in shame
knowing
I have never
ever
had a single
excuse
to miss
even one sujood
yet I have missed
many.

UNSHACKLED

I once saw the world in colours
hues
tints
but now there is only red
once a shade of love
now
the shade of blood
smeared on the hands of hundreds
marked for eternal destruction.

UNSHACKLED

I thought we were at the pinnacle
of civility
the height of modern enlightenment
but the father roaming around
distressed
collecting burnt
unrecognizable
body parts
of his only son
in a plastic bag
he had found on the streets
humbled me
        shamed me
                silenced me
                        broke me.

UNSHACKLED

What more can they show us?
what more can our eyes see?
what more can they display?
what more can our hearts bear?
what is there left to say?
what is there left to witness?

Humanity you have failed.

Humanity you have failed.

UNSHACKLED

You celebrate
as you render my body
lifeless
laying on the dirt
atop my slaughtered brother
you think we're done for
but we still linger
in your subconscious
in every fiber of your body
because our souls that you cannot destroy
will haunt you in ways you could never imagine
in this life
and the next
you will be forced to remember
you have wronged yourselves
before you have wronged our lives
and what you sow
you will
always
always
always
reap.

SANA MALIM

UNSHACKLED

I see him
smile cheek to cheek
bragging about his search
for more children to murder
for more babies to kill
I am left crippled
wondering
how a people can become so
shameless
heinous
wicked
perverse
evil to the naked core
and still believe
enough in Gods' mercy
to call themselves
the chosen ones.

UNSHACKLED

Sweet little boy
your tiny fingers still wrapped around
the white flag you carried
when you arrive at Allah's throne
and ask your culprits
for what crime
a bullet was fired
through your short years of innocence
I pray
with every tear I have cried
over your lifeless body
the gaping hole in your forehead
that I am there
to witness your smiles
your limitless laughter
to witness your peace
your calm
as you embrace your father
your mother
your infant sister
on the day that justice is delivered
to all of creation
for earth did not deserve
an angel like you.

SANA MALIM

UNSHACKLED

I never knew it was this hard
to convince the world
that children don't deserve to die
horrific unimaginable deaths
or suffer violent atrocities
that kill their
past, present, and future.

I never knew it was this hard
to convince the world that children should never
have to watch their parents, siblings, friends
burn to the bone
bleed to death.

I never knew it was this hard
to convince the world
to do something
anything
to prevent the bodies of children
from decomposing on the streets.

I never knew it was this hard
to convince the world
of their moral duties
that talking about saving children was controversial
that we'd have to stay silent
become spectators
to keep the illusionary peace.

I never knew it was this hard
to convince the world
that children begging for their life
or wishing to die with the murdered
was a cataclysmic tragedy
that no human should ever have to bear.
I never knew.

SANA MALIM

UNSHACKLED

The colour of your skin
the faith in your heart
is enough reason
for you to be
robbed
killed
bombed
destroyed.

This is the tale
I am forced to tell my children
who don't yet understand
hatred
but they must be made aware
before they are shown
that the colour of your skin
and the faith in your heart
is enough reason
for you to be
abandoned
and erased.

UNSHACKLED

I've fallen out of love with you
I don't see the charm anymore
I don't feel the warmth anymore.

I only see
rivers made of tears
clouds made of smoke
trees turned into dust
homes turned into ashes
people turned into graves
hearts turned into rocks.

How did I ever mistake
your lies
for truth?
your illusions
for beauty?

I've fallen out of love with you
world
I no longer see the charm in you.

SANA MALIM

UNSHACKLED

When will they learn
a soul does not choose
the body it ends up in
the colour it is wrapped in
the faith it is entwined in.

A soul does not choose
it is simply
sent
so how then
do people decide
so easily
which souls do not deserve
a body
a life
a chance?

UNSHACKLED

All my life
I was told
I was barbaric
for covering my head
for draping my body
for believing in Muhammad [peace be upon him]
for loving Allah
yet
I have watched in silence
since my adolescence
leaders of the free world
of the civilized world
build mountains
of limbs
of bones
of corpses
and still
all my life
I was told
I was the one
who was barbaric.

UNSHACKLED

Shall I tell you
what is wrong with a world
where families pray their hardest
to be killed together
in an instant
intact
in one piece
in recognizable states
preferably in their homes
but really
anywhere
they can be found
and buried?

Words escape me
so my heart replies
                "everything."

UNSHACKLED

What a shame
that there is an infinite amount of wealth in the world
available within seconds
to bomb
slaughter
destroy children
but never enough
to feed
clothe
or house them.

UNSHACKLED

I've come to the conclusion that
there are no words
that can be thought
that can be spoken
that can do justice
that can suffice
that can be satisfactory to a wailing heart
that can be accurately used to describe
the depth of pain that is felt
when a soul is killed
before the body has died
because language
was not meant
to describe such evil
because people
were not meant
to be such demons.

UNSHACKLED

It's like
my eyes have dried
my tongue has gone silent
my heart has numbed
my body has gone cold.

It's like
I have died
but I am still living
plunged into perpetual paralysis
watching
every human being who can stop this madness
indulge in it.

UNSHACKLED

Do you see now?

That governments
don't act in the people's best interests
don't act out of goodness
don't act to protect people
don't act to uphold the law?

That governments
don't care for the sanctity of life
whether of their own citizens
or abroad?

They would spill blood
again and again and again
repeat history
a thousand times over
because
the soul-less only ever speak
the language of
greed.

Do you see now?

UNSHACKLED

These screams
that are music to your sickly ears
ignite
with every frequency
the blazing flames of your eternal dwelling.

UNSHACKLED

Twisted tongues
cannot pronounce

ceasefire

they only enjoy
a drink called
blood.

The Flour Massacre

If only they knew
that they'd be forced
to use
their own blood
to knead the dough
of the bread
their families await.

UNSHACKLED

When the world's most powerful military
with all of its riches and all of its arms
is defeated by a
starved
weapon-less
oppressed people
the world will not pity the tyrants
the world will only cheer.

Never forget to say
Free Palestine

-Motaz Azaiza

Glossary

Allah	God
Allah Hu Akbar	Allah is the Greatest
Alhumdulilah	Praise be to God
Falasteen	Palestine
Hasbunallah Wa Ni'mal Wakeel	Sufficient for us is Allah, and [He is] the best disposer of affairs.
Imaan	Faith
Innallaaha Ma As Saabireen	Surely, Allah is with those who are patient
Innalilahi Wa Inna Ilayhi Raji'oon	To Allah we belong, and to Him is our return.
Qadr	Divine decree
Jannah	Paradise
Jahannum	Hell
Sujood	The act of lowering your forehead to the ground in prayer

About The Author

Sana Malim is a writer, poet, and children's book author on a journey to increase Muslim representation in mainstream literature. She currently resides in Toronto, Canada, with her beloved husband and children. To learn more about her, connect with her on social media @sanaimalim.

www.ingramcontent.com/pod-product-compliance
Lightning Source LLC
Chambersburg PA
CBHW042130100526
44587CB00026B/4250